Listening Advantage

Tom Kenny
Tamami Wada

THOMSON

HEINLE

Australia · Canada · Mexico · Singapore · Spain · United Kingdom · United States

THOMSON

HEINLE

Listening Advantage, Student Book 1
Kenny / Wada

Publisher: Christopher Wenger
Director of Content Development: Anita Raducanu
Director of Product Marketing: Amy Mabley
Editorial Manager: Sean Bermingham
Development Editor: Derek Mackrell
Production Editor: Tan Jin Hock
International Marketing Manager: Ian Martin

Sr. Print Buyer: Mary Beth Hennebury
Compositor: CHROME Media Pte. Ltd.
Illustrator: Edwin Ng
Cover/Text Designer: CHROME Media Pte. Ltd.
Printer: Transcontinental
Cover Images: CHROME Media Photodisc, Inc.

For more information contact Thomson Heinle, 25 Thomson Place, Boston, Massachusetts 02210 USA. You can visit our web site at elt.thomson.com

Printed in Canada.
1 2 3 4 5 6 7 8 9 10   11 10 09 08 07

Student Book ISBN-13: 978-1-4240-0197-2
Student Book ISBN-10: 1-4240-0197-8
Book + Audio CD ISBN-13: 978-1-4240-0175-0
Book + Audio CD ISBN-10: 1-4240-0175-7

Photo Credits
Landov: pages 8 (top), 11; Photos.com: pages 7 (top right), 8 (bottom all), 12 (top left and center, bottom), 18 (all except far right), 20 (top center), 22 (all except center left), 24, 25, 26 (1st three from left), 28 (bottom), 30 (top row 2nd from left and bottom row center left), 31, 38, 46, 48 (bottom all), 49, 50 (all except center and 2nd from right), 51 (bottom), 52 (center row), 54, 56, 58 (top row all and bottom row center right), 59; Index Open: pages 7 (top left and second row right) 12 (top right), 18 (far right), 29 (top row except far right), 50 (center), 58 (center left); iStockphoto: pages 7 (second row left and bottom three), 15, 20 (top left, top right, bottom left), 26 (far right), 27, page 30 (top row center), 48 (top), 51 (top), 52 (top row and bottom row), 58 (far left and far right), 68; Photo Objects: pages 20 (bottom center and bottom right), 28 (top row all), 28 (top far right and bottom all), page 30 (all except top row center and 2nd from left and bottom row center left), 42; HIRB: pages 22 (center left), 26 (2nd from right), 50 (2nd from right)

The authors and publisher would like to thank the following reviewers for their help during the development of this series:
Mike Bryan, Nihon University Junior/Senior High School; **David Buchanan,** St. Dominic High School; **Hsin-Hwa Chen,** Yuan Ze University; **Wong Fook Fei,** Universiti Kebangsaan; **Ding Guocheng,** Shanghai Jincai Middle School; **Caroline C. Hwang,** National Taipei University of Technology; **Michelle Misook Kim,** Kyung Hee University; **Young Hee Cheri Lee,** Reading Town USA English Language Institute**; Hae Chin Moon,** Korea University; **Chieko Okada,** Toho Senior High School; **Hiromi Okamura,** Toho Senior High School; **Kate Mastruserio Reynolds,** University of Wisconsin - Eau Claire; **Yoshi Sato,** Nagoya University of Foreign Studies; **Joe Spear,** Hanbat National University; **Keiko Takahashi,** Ikeda Senior High School; **Yanan Une-aree,** Bangkok University; **Mei-ling Wu,** Mackay Medicine, Nursing and Management College

Contents

Scope and Sequence

Daily Life

Unit	Lesson	Language/Strategy	Catch It!
1 Names and Addresses *Page 8*	**A** How do you spell that? **B** What's your e-mail address?	• Basic phrases • Showing you're listening	Spelling out words
2 Numbers *Page 12*	**A** Can I have your number? **B** I'm free on the 14th at 7 o'clock.	• Requesting information • Repeating	Syllable stress
3 Going Places *Page 16*	**A** How do you get there? **B** What do you do after school?	• Adverbs of frequency • Showing understanding	Sentence stress

Places and Things

Unit	Lesson	Language/Strategy	Catch It!
4 Locations *Page 20*	**A** Where is it? **B** How do you get there?	• Prepositional phrases • Clarifying directions	Weak forms of prepositions
5 Likes and Dislikes *Page 24*	**A** What's your favorite? **B** Good idea!	• Rejoinders • Showing agreement and disagreement	Weak forms of *would you / do you + like*
6 My Stuff *Page 28*	**A** Nice shirt! **B** How much?	• Giving and receiving compliments • Reacting to prices	Reduced pronouns

People I Know

Unit	Lesson	Language/Strategy	Catch It!
7 Home Life *Page 38*	**A** My dad's a salesman. **B** Wow, you have a lot of CDs!	• Yes/no questions • Introducing a question with "So, . . . "	Intonation for questions
8 Classmates *Page 42*	**A** What's he look like? **B** Is that in fashion?	• Comparing people • Repeating the question	Breaking sentences into chunks
9 Best Friends *Page 46*	**A** Chuck's a really cool guy! **B** What's she like?	• *like/enjoy* + verb • Getting time to think	The sound / θ /

Hopes and Dreams

Unit	Lesson	Language/Strategy	Catch It!
10 Holidays *Page 50*	**A** Let's go! **B** I really like winter!	• Inviting • Returning a question	*What/How about you?*
11 Dating *Page 54*	**A** What kind of guy? **B** How about dinner and a movie?	• Accepting and refusing invitations • Making suggestions	*Can* vs. *can't*
12 My Future *Page 58*	**A** I want to be a TV star! **B** You get three wishes!	• *Hope/want* + *to* . . . • Showing excitement	Reduced forms of *want to* and *going to*

Introduction

Listening in a foreign language is sometimes very difficult. People talk very fast and they use a lot of words and difficult language. *Listening Advantage* will help you!

Real situations and interesting topics

Listening Advantage uses situations from real life:

People in *Listening Advantage* talk about interesting things:

Useful language and pronunciation practice

Language Focus will teach you useful language from real life.

Catch It! will help you understand the way that English speakers talk.

Important strategies

Conversation Strategy sections show you how to listen more actively.

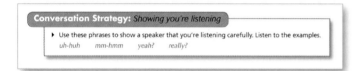

Practice your strategies in the *Talk It Over* and *Try It Out!* sections.

Test taking skills

The *Self-Study* section and *Practice Tests* give lots of listening test practice.

To become a good listener, listen as much as you can—in class and outside class. We hope you enjoy using *Listening Advantage*! Good luck!

Tom and Tamami

Useful Expressions

Could you repeat that, please?

Sorry, I don't understand.

What does this mean?

What's your answer for question 1?

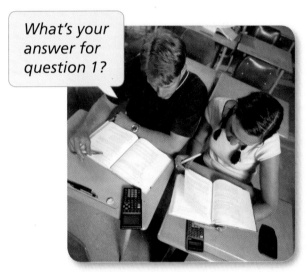

Could you turn up the volume, please?

How do you spell that?

More slowly, please.

Names and Addresses

Lesson A   *How do you spell that?*

Warm-up

A   Here are the names of six famous people. What letters are missing from their names? Listen.

1   Eric <u>B</u>ana
2   Or__ando B__oom
3   B__ad Pitt
4   Jenni__er __ope__
5   Jackie __ __ an
6   __ince __aughn
7   __atherine __eta-Jones
8   Tom __ruise

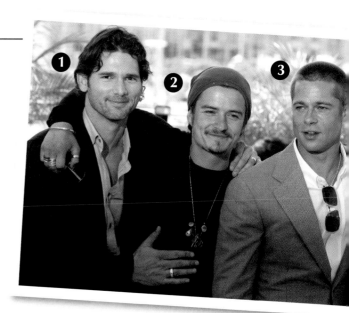

B   Listen again and check your answers. Say the names to a partner.

Listening

A   Four speakers are talking about where they live. Listen and number the pictures 1–4.

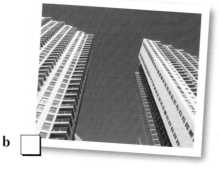

a ▢
b ▢
c ▢
d ▢

B   Listen again. Complete the addresses.

1   816 _____ Street
2   25 _____ Circle
3   1 _____ Court
4   2902 _____ Street

Further Listening

 A Four people are making reservations at a restaurant. Listen and number the reservations 1–4.

VISTA DE NADA RESTAURANT

Time	Name
Lunch	
12:30	_____
1:00	Ende
1:30	Lanes
2:00	Benett
Dinner	
6:00	Simons
6:30	_____

 B Listen again. Correct the mistakes in the names.

Language Focus: *Basic phrases*

▸ When you don't understand what a speaker says, use these phrases:

How do you spell that?	*One more time, please.*	*More slowly, please.*
Could you repeat that?	*Could you say that again?*	

 C Listen again. Check (✔) the phrases you hear.

	1	2	3	4
How do you spell that?				
One more time, please.				
More slowly, please.				

Talk It Over

Work with a partner. Choose a famous person from the Warm-up on page 6 or another person. Ask your partner for his or her name and write it down.

Partner A _____

Partner B _____

What's your name?

Orlando Bloom.

How do you spell that?

O-R-L-A-N-D-O B-L-O-O-M

Lesson B *What's your e-mail address?*

Before You Listen

A   Answer these questions. Circle **yes** or **no**.

1 I have an e-mail address.	yes no	**3** I sometimes go to an Internet café.	yes no
2 I have my own web page.	yes no	**4** I have used the Internet for chat.	yes no

B   Look at this URL (web address). Write the name of each symbol, using the words in the box. Listen and check your answers.

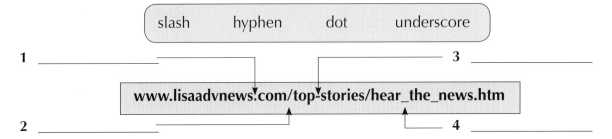

slash   hyphen   dot   underscore

1 _____

3 _____

www.lisaadvnews.com/top-stories/hear_the_news.htm

2 _____

4 _____

Extended Listening

A   Four people are talking about e-mail and the Internet. Listen and number the pictures 1–4.

B   Listen again. Write the address under each picture.

Conversation Strategy: *Showing you're listening*

▸ Use these phrases to show a speaker that you're listening carefully. Listen to the examples.

uh-huh   mm-hmm   yeah?   really?

C   Listen again. How many times is each phrase used. Check (✔).

	1	2	3	4
uh-huh				
mm-hmm				
yeah?				
really?				

Catch It!: Spelling out words

 A   When you spell out a word or name,
your tone should go down on the last letter.
Listen to the example.

J-A-C-K-I-E C-H-A-N

 B   Listen to the speakers spell their names.
Write the names on the lines below.

1 _____

2 _____

3 _____

4 _____

5 _____

Try It Out!

Write your e-mail address and the URL of two websites you like in the table.
Work with two partners. Ask your partners questions and fill in the rest of the table.

A: What's your e-mail address?

B: It's megumi_123@yahoo.co.jp.

A: What's a website that you like?

B: I like imdb.com.

A: Really? What's another website
you like?

B: I also like myspace.com.

	e-mail address	website 1	website 2
Me			
Partner 1			
Partner 2			

Numbers

Can I have your number?

Warm-up

A Look at the numbers in the box. Listen.

> 0, 1, 2, 3, 4, 5, 6, 7, 8, 9, 10, 11, 12, 13, 17,
> 19, 27, 39, 78, 100, 145, 451, 835, 904

B Let's play bingo! Write a number from A in each space on the Bingo form. Listen and check (✔) the numbers you hear. If you have four in a row, shout "Bingo!"

Bingo!

Listening

A Four people are talking about places. Listen and number the pictures 1–4.

a

b

c

B Listen again and circle the correct number.

| 1 | a 75 | b 175 | 3 | a 1067 | b 167 |
| 2 | a 2439 | b 2349 | 4 | a 278 | b 287 |

d

12

Further Listening

 A   Listen to four conversations. Number the pictures 1–4.

a ☐   b ☐   c ☐   d ☐

 B   Listen again. Write the numbers you hear.

1 _____   2 _____   3 _____   4 _____

Language Focus: *Requesting information*

▸ Use these phrases to ask for information.

What's your home telephone number?   **Can I have** your cell phone number, please?
Can you give me your fax number?

C   Listen again. Check (✔) the phrases you hear.

	1	2	3	4
What's?				
Can I have?				
Can you give me?				

Talk It Over

Work with two partners. Ask your partners for their phone numbers and write them down.

Partner A _____

Partner B _____

What's your home number?

What's your cell phone number?

Before You Listen

A Match the words with the numbers in the box. Listen.

1st	2nd	3rd	4th	5th	6th	7th	8th	9th	10th
11th	12th	13th	14th	20th	21st	22nd	23rd	30th	31st

second _____   fourth _____   thirty-first _____   fifth _____
seventh _____   twenty-second _____ thirtieth _____   first _____
eighth _____   tenth _____   twenty-first _____   twelfth _____
thirteenth _____   twentieth _____   eleventh _____   third _____
sixth _____   twenty-third _____   ninth _____   fourteenth _____

B Here are the months of the year. Number them 1–12. Listen.

				1	
September	February	December	March	January	June
May	August	April	October	July	November

C Work with a partner. What date is it today? What date is your birthday?

Today's date _____   My birthday _____

Extended Listening

A Listen to four conversations about making plans. Number the activities 1–4.

movie ___   dentist ___   study ___   picnic ___

B Kan is filling in his schedule book. Listen again. What will he do this month, and when?
Write the activities from A next to the date, along with their time. The first one has been
done for you.

Sunday	Monday	Tuesday	Wednesday	Thursday	Friday	Saturday
			1	2	3	4
5	6	7	8	9 Dentist 4:15	10	11
12	13	14	15	16	17	18

▸ Listeners often repeat what they hear to check if it's right. Listen to the examples:

Example 1: 7:15 ⟍↗   **Example 2:** 7:15 ⟋↗

In Example 1, the listener's not sure. In Example 2, the listener is sure it's right.

C   Listen to the conversations again. When the speaker repeats, is the speaker sure or not sure? Circle the answer below.

1	sure	not sure	**3**	sure	not sure
2	sure	not sure	**4**	sure	not sure

Catch It!: Syllable stress

 A   Listen to how these numbers are pronounced.

13	thirTEEN	30	THIRty
13th	thirTEENTH	30th	THIRtieth

 B   Listen to the sentences and circle the correct answer.

1	**a** 14th	**b** 40th		**4**	**a** 15	**b** 50
2	**a** 13th	**b** 30th		**5**	**a** 17	**b** 70
3	**a** 18th	**b** 80th		**6**	**a** 16	**b** 60

Try It Out!

What time do you do the activities below? Write your answers in the table. Ask two partners what time they do the activities.

Example:

A: What time do you wake up?

B: I wake up at 6:15.

A: 6:50?

B: No. 6:15.

A: When do you get home?

B: At 4 o'clock.

What time do you . . . ?	Me	Partner 1	Partner 2
wake up			
have breakfast			
get to school			
get home			
have dinner			
go to bed			

Going Places

Lesson A   *How do you get there?*

Warm-up

A How are the people going to school? Label the picture using the words from the box. Listen and check.

1 _____

by bus	by train
by car	by bike
on foot	

2 _____

3 _____

4 _____   5 _____

HIG SCHO

B Complete these sentences with your own information. Tell your partner.

I usually go to school _____.   I usually go to _____ house _____.

I usually go to _____ _____.   *my friend's name*

name of store

Listening

A Listen to four conversations. Circle the correct picture for each one.

❶ a   b

❷ a   b

❸ a   b

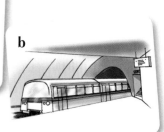

❹ a   b

B   Listen again. How long does each speaker's journey take?

1	**a** 1 hour	**b** 2 hours	**3**	**a** 4 or 5 minutes	**b** 45 minutes
2	**a** 5 minutes	**b** 50 minutes	**4**	**a** 15 minutes	**b** 50 minutes

Further Listening

 A   Five speakers are talking about going to school. Listen and number the illustrations 1–5.

a   b   c   d   e

Language Focus: *Adverbs of frequency*

▸ People use these words to show how often they do something:

   always   usually   often   sometimes   never

B   Listen again. Which adverbs do the speakers use? Check (✔) the boxes.

	always	usually	often	sometimes	never
1					
2					
3					
4					
5					

Talk It Over

Complete these sentences with your own information.

I go to school _____.

It _____ takes _____.

How do you go to school?

How long does it take?

What do you do after school?

Before You Listen

A Match the activities in the box to the correct picture.

> hanging out with friends   shopping   riding a bike   studying   watching movies

a _____ b _____ c _____ d _____ e _____

B Which of the activities above do you like? Number them 1–5. (1 = like the most)

Extended listening

 A Three people are applying for a job at a video rental store. What does each person like to do? Listen to the three interviews and choose the correct pictures.

1 Megumi

a

b

2 Kirk

a

b

3

a

Yoon-Hee

b

 B Listen again. Which person got the job?

    a Megumi   **b** Kirk   **c** Yoon-Hee

▸ Use these phrases to show you understand what someone is saying.

OK.   I see.   Alright.   Got it.

C Listen again. What phrases does the interviewer use?

	1	2	3
OK.			
I see.			
Alright.			
Got it.			

Catch It!: Sentence Stress

A Listen to how the speaker places stress in these questions.

HOW do you COME to SCHOOL?   How OFTEN are you LATE?
How LONG does it TAKE?

B Listen to the sentences and underline the stressed words.

1 How often do you do homework?
2 What time do you go home?
3 How often do you talk with your friends?

4 How often do you take the bus?
5 How long does it take to get home?
6 What time do you eat breakfast?

Try It Out!

Read and answer these questions. Write two more questions. Then ask your partner.

Example:

A: How do you come to school?
B: I usually come to school by bus.
A: I see.

A: How long does it take?
B: About 30 minutes.
A: OK.

A: How often are you late?
B: I'm <u>never</u> late.
A: Really?

Activity	Me	My partner
How do you come to school?	*by bus*	
How long does it take?		
How often are you late?		
How often do you do homework?		
How often do you ride the bus?		
How often . . . ?		
How often . . . ?		

Locations

4

Warm-up

  A Complete the sentences using the words in the box.
Listen and check.

Max   Sophia

Marco

Yoon-Hee

> **a** behind **b** next to **c** in front of

1 Marco sits _____ Max.
2 Sophia sits _____ Yoon-Hee.
3 Yoon-Hee sits _____ Marco.

B Where do you sit in class? Complete the sentences and compare with a partner.

I sit behind _____.   I sit next to _____.   I sit in front of _____.

Listening

  A Five people are talking about things they like. Listen and number them 1–5.
One thing is not used.

a ☐

b ☐

c ☐

d ☐

e ☐

f ☐

B Listen again. Where is each item? Circle the correct answer.

1 **a** on the shelf   **b** next to the shelf   4 **a** on the wall   **b** on the bed
2 **a** in my pocket   **b** next to the stereo   5 **a** behind my bag   **b** in my bag
3 **a** in the corner   **b** behind the computer

Further Listening

A Five people are asking for directions. Listen. Where does each person want to go? One place is extra.

convenience store ___   book store ___
taxi stand ___   game center ___
bus stop ___   spy HQ ___

B Listen again. Where is each place?
Number the buildings 1–5.

Language Focus: *Prepositional phrases*

▶ Use prepositional phrases to describe the location of things and people. Here are some examples:

   on the street   *across from* the post office   *next to* the store   *on* the corner

C Listen again. Write the prepositions you hear.

a _____ the coffee shop   **c** _____ the corner   **e** _____ the supermarket
b _____ the bank   **d** _____ the big fountain

Talk It Over

Work with two partners.
Ask about the location of things in the classroom.
Answer your partners' questions.

Where's your cell phone?

It's in my bag.

How do you get there?

Before You Listen

A Look at the route on the map. Number the directions 1–4. Listen and check.

a Go straight at the corner. ____   **c** Turn left at the signal. ____
b Turn left after the bookstore. ____   **d** Go to the bank and turn right. ____

B Practice describing the route to your partner.

Extended Listening

A Four people are asking Sung-Taek for directions. Where do they want to go?
Number the places 1–4.

a The post office is on the (right / left).

b The restaurant is (between / near) the library and the photo shop.

c The subway station is (across from / around the corner from) the shopping center.

d The shopping center is (under / next to) Green Park.

B Listen again. Where is each place? Circle the correct answer.

▸ Use *what* or *where* to ask a speaker to clarify their directions. For example:

A: Go down the street, turn right, and it's on the left.
B: Go down the street, turn where?
A: Turn right.
B: Got it.

A: After the bookstore, turn left at the light.
B: After the what?
A: The bookstore.
B: OK.

 C Listen again. How does the person ask Sung-Taek to clarify? Circle the word.

1 **a** where **b** what   2 **a** where **b** what   3 **a** where **b** what   4 **a** where **b** what

Catch It!: Weak forms of prepositions

A Prepositions can be hard to catch because they are usually not stressed. Listen to the example. Did she say *at* or *in*?

I'll meet you (at)/ in) the post office.

 B Listen. Which preposition does the speaker use? Complete the sentences.

1 _____ the street
2 _____ the post office
3 _____ the road

4 _____ the station
5 _____ the corner
6 _____ the bridge

Try It Out!

Work with a partner. Decide who is A and who is B.

Student A: Label your places (the police station, the supermarket, the game center, the department store, the hospital) on the green parts of the map.

Student B: Label your places (the post office, the drug store, the coffee shop, the bookstore, the bus stop) on the red parts of the map. Ask your partner where each of his or her places is. Label them on the map.

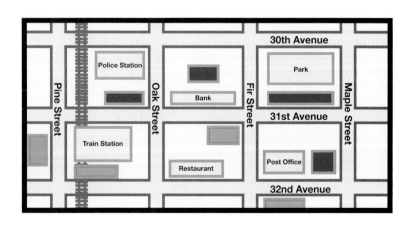

Likes and Dislikes 5

Warm-up

 A Look at the words in the box. Is each word a season, a fruit, a drink, or a color? Write **S, F, D,** or **C** next to each one. Listen and check.

F apple	winter	red	tea	banana	spring	blue	juice	peach	summer
yellow	cola	grape	fall	green	milk	coffee	orange	purple	watermelon

B What are your favorites? Tell a partner.

> My favorite season is winter.

Listening

A Four speakers are talking about what they like. Number the topics 1–4.

   a _____ fruit   **b** _____ seasons   **c** _____ drinks   **d** _____ colors

B Which does each speaker like best? Circle it.

a   b

a   b

a   b

a   b

Further Listening

A   Listen to five conversations. Some friends are talking about what they like and dislike. What is each conversation about?

☐   ☐   ☐   ☐   ☐

B   Listen again. Do the speakers like (✔) or dislike (✗) each thing? Complete the chart.

	1	2	3	4	5
Speaker 1					
Speaker 2					

Language Focus: *Rejoinders*

▶ Use these phrases to agree or disagree with someone.

Agree		Disagree	
A: I don't like fruit.	**B:** Me neither.	**A:** I like fruit.	**B:** Uh, I don't.
A: I like winter.	**B:** Me too.	**A:** I don't like winter.	**B:** Really? I do.

C   Circle the words the speakers use to agree or disagree.

1 **a** me too **b** me neither   3 **a** I do   **b** I don't   5 **a** I do **b** I don't
2 **a** me too **b** me neither   4 **a** me too **b** me neither

Talk It Over

Work with a partner. Tell your partner about things you like or dislike. Your partner will agree or disagree.

I like homework.

Really? I don't.

Lesson B *Good idea!*

Before You Listen

🎧 **A**   Match the activity to the picture. Listen and check.

| playing video games   reading a book   singing karaoke   taking a test   watching movies |

a _____   b _____   c _____   d _____   e _____

B   How much do you enjoy each activity above? Check (✔) the boxes below.

	Really like	Like	Don't like	Can't stand
1 playing video games				
2 reading a book				
3 singing karaoke				
4 taking a test				
5 watching movies				

Extended Listening

🎧 **A**   Two friends are deciding what to do. Listen and number the activities they talk about 1–4.

1 ☐   2 ☐   3 ☐   4 ☐

a nice weather **a** stereo is broken **a** no new comics **a** no money
b no homework **b** no bands playing **b** comics are boring **b** no time

🎧 **B**   Listen again. What is the problem with each suggestion? Circle the correct problem.

▶ Use these phrases to show you agree with someone's idea.

That's great.   Good idea.

▶ Use these phrases to show you disagree.

I'm not sure.   No way!

C Circle the phrase the speaker uses in each conversation.

1 a No way.	**a** Good idea.	**3 a** I'm not sure. **b** No way.
2 a That's great.	**b** I'm not sure.	**4 a** Good idea. **b** That's great.

Catch It!: Weak forms of *would you/do you + like*

A Listen to how "would you" and "do you" are pronounced in spoken English. Practice saying these sentences with a partner.

Do you like to go bowling?   Would you like to go bowling?

B Listen again. Does the speaker say "would you" or "do you"? Circle the correct answer.

1	do you	would you	**5**	do you	would you
2	do you	would you	**6**	do you	would you
3	do you	would you	**7**	do you	would you
4	do you	would you			

Try It Out!

Look at the activities in the table and add three of your own. Ask your classmates to join your activity. They will agree or disagree. Write the names of three people who want to join you.

A: Would you like to play tennis?
B: Play tennis? No way!
A: Would you like to play tennis?
C: Good idea!

I want to	Classmates' names
play tennis	_____
see a movie	_____
sing karaoke	_____
_____	_____
_____	_____
_____	_____

My Stuff

6

Lesson A *Nice shirt!*

Warm-up

 A Use the words to label the pictures. One is extra. Listen and check.

| T-shirt   skirt   sweater   jeans   bracelet   blouse |

1 _____   2 _____   3 _____   4 _____   5 _____

B Which do you wear? How often? Check (✔) your answers and compare with your partner.

	T-shirt	skirt	sweater	jeans	bracelet	blouse
everyday						
often						
sometimes						
never						

Listening

 A Listen. Number the items in the order you hear them.

a shoes _____   **c** blouse _____   **e** bag _____

b watch _____   **d** sweater _____

 B What information do the speakers give about each item?
Match the description to the item.

1 not so comfortable _____   **4** for cold days _____

2 matches everything _____   **5** have it in yellow and blue _____

3 matches my belt _____

Further Listening

A People are talking about their friends' clothes. Match the description to the item.

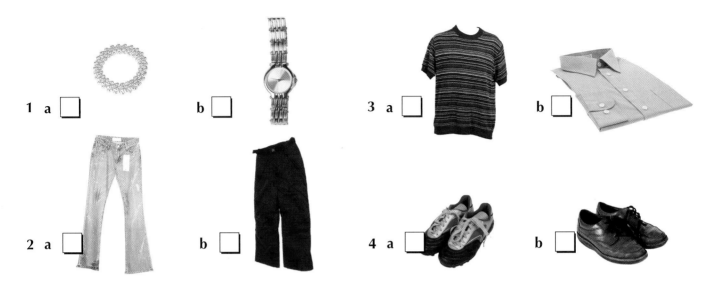

1 a ☐   b ☐   3 a ☐   b ☐

2 a ☐   b ☐   4 a ☐   b ☐

Language Focus: *Giving and receiving compliments*

▶ People use phrases like these to compliment—to say they like something someone is wearing:

  Nice shirt!   **Cool** jeans!   *Cute* sweater!

▶ To receive a compliment, say "Thank you" and then give some extra information:

• Thanks.	It was a present from _____.
• Thank you.	(person)
	It's old / new.
	I got it at _____.
	(place)

B Listen again. Which phrases for giving a compliment do you hear?
What information does the other person give? Check (✔) the words.

	Giving			Receiving		
	nice	cool	cute	present	old / new	where
1						
2						
3						
4						

Talk It Over

Work with two partners. Compliment
your partners about their shirts, bags,
and two other things.

Nice shirt.

Thanks, it was a present.

Before You Listen

A Look at the items. Rank them from 1 (cheapest) to 5 (most expensive) in the boxes.

B Which of these would you like to have the most? Tell your partner.

I want the laptop computer. How about you?

I really want the cool bicycle.

Extended Listening

 A Andrew and Keiko are shopping for the perfect gift. Number the items 1–4.

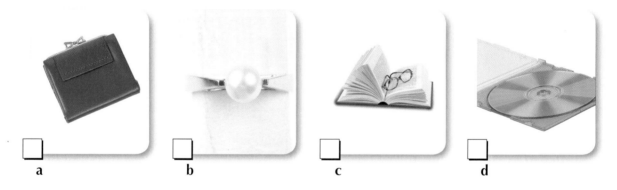

a   b   c   d

 B Listen again. What do they decide to buy?

> **Conversation Strategy:** *Reacting to prices*
>
> ▸ People sometimes use simple phrases to react to prices when shopping:
> *Good price.*   *That's very cheap.*   *Oh, too expensive.*

C Listen again. Keiko and Andrew agree about the items. Circle the phrases they use.

1   Good price!   very cheap   too expensive
2   Good price!   very cheap   too expensive
3   Good price!   very cheap   too expensive
4   Good price!   very cheap   too expensive

Catch It!: Reduced pronouns

A Pronouns are words like his, her, my, and yours. Speakers usually don't stress pronouns, so they're often hard to catch! Listen to the example. Does the speaker say his or her?

> *That's his/her sweater on the shelf.*

B Listen to the sentences. Circle the pronoun the speaker uses.

1 his   her
2 her   your
3 him   them
4 him   them
5 him   her
6 her   their

Try It Out!

Look at the items on the shelves. You and your partner are shopping. Circle three items you like and let your partner circle three different items. Decide on a price for the three items you chose. Then talk about each item like this:

A: I like that T-shirt.
   How much is it?
B: It's six dollars and fifty cents.
A: Oh, that's very cheap.

B: I like that MP3 player.
   How much is it?
A: It's five hundred dollars.
B: Oh, that's too expensive.

Practice Test

Part 1

Listen. Choose the best answer.

1 Where does the woman live now?

a

c

b

d

2 What website is he looking at now?

a

c

b

d

3 What is his cell phone number?

    a 984-239-4483   **b** 984-329-4483   **c** 980-239-4483   **d** 980-329-4483

4 What time did the class start this morning?

    a 8:15   **b** 8:30   **c** 8:45   **d** 8:50

5 How does he go to school?

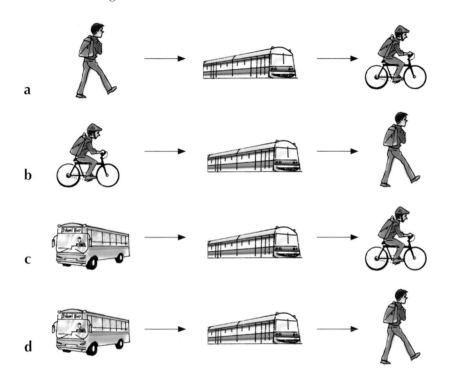

6 Where is the coffee shop?

Listen. Choose the best reply.

7   **a** No I don't know.   **b** Thank you.   **c** I like it.   **d** No, thank you.

8   **a** Around 6:45.   **b** I think so.   **c** It's very good.   **d** It was 3:40.

9   **a** So where did you go to school?   **c** So did you arrive early?
    b So why did you go to school?   **d** So how did you go to school?

10 **a** What time did you go to bed?   **c** How many times did you call?
    b How did you go to bed?   **d** What time did you call?

11 **a** Really? Oh, you can walk there.   **c** Really? Oh, you can take the subway.
    b Really? Oh, you can go by car.   **d** Really? Oh, you can take the bus.

12 **a** Her name is Naomi.   **b** She likes yellow.   **c** Her bag is cute.   **d** She is singing.

13 **a** I don't like it.   **b** I like to do it.   **c** It is 8:00.   **d** I do it before dinner.

Part 3

A Listen. Choose the best answer.

14 Which bus does the man take?

    a Bus three   **b** Bus thirty   **c** Bus thirteen   **d** Bus fifty

15 What is the woman's e-mail address?

    a kepri@oel.com   **b** kipri@eol.com   **c** kepri@eol.com   **d** kipre@oel.com

16 What are they going to do now?

    a sing a song   **b** work on the computer   **c** play computer games   **d** go to the zoo

B Listen. Choose the best answer (a–f) for questions 17–19.

Schedule

Monday	Tuesday	Wednesday	Thursday	Friday	Saturday	Sunday
		17		18	19	

    a Tennis practice   **d** Going to see a movie

    b Baseball practice   **e** Free in the morning

    c Piano lesson   **f** Free all day

Part 4

A   Listen. Choose the best answer.

20 What time does the class usually begin?

    a 9:15   **b** 8:45   **c** 8:30   **d** 8:15

21 In total, how many hours is she going to use the Internet next week?

    a 1 hour   **b** 2 hours   **c** 4 hours   **d** 7 hours

22 How many English lessons does she have outside of school every week?

    a two   **b** three   **c** five   **d** seven

B   Listen. Choose the best answer.

23 How do many American students go to school?

    a in a friend's car   **b** by city bus   **c** by school bus   **d** by train

24 At what age can most people in America get a driver's license?

    a 15 years old   **b** 16 years old   **c** 17 years old   **d** 18 years old

25 Where do most American students take driving lessons?

    a at home   **b** at driving school   **c** in high school   **d** in a car

Practice Test 1 Answer Sheet

Part 1

1 ⓐ ⓑ ⓒ ⓓ   4 ⓐ ⓑ ⓒ ⓓ

2 ⓐ ⓑ ⓒ ⓓ   5 ⓐ ⓑ ⓒ ⓓ

3 ⓐ ⓑ ⓒ ⓓ   6 ⓐ ⓑ ⓒ ⓓ

Part 2

7 ⓐ ⓑ ⓒ ⓓ   11 ⓐ ⓑ ⓒ ⓓ

8 ⓐ ⓑ ⓒ ⓓ   12 ⓐ ⓑ ⓒ ⓓ

9 ⓐ ⓑ ⓒ ⓓ   13 ⓐ ⓑ ⓒ ⓓ

10 ⓐ ⓑ ⓒ ⓓ

Part 3

14 ⓐ ⓑ ⓒ ⓓ   17 ⓐ ⓑ ⓒ ⓓ ⓔ ⓕ

15 ⓐ ⓑ ⓒ ⓓ   18 ⓐ ⓑ ⓒ ⓓ ⓔ ⓕ

16 ⓐ ⓑ ⓒ ⓓ   19 ⓐ ⓑ ⓒ ⓓ ⓔ ⓕ

Part 4

A   **B**

20 ⓐ ⓑ ⓒ ⓓ   23 ⓐ ⓑ ⓒ ⓓ

21 ⓐ ⓑ ⓒ ⓓ   24 ⓐ ⓑ ⓒ ⓓ

22 ⓐ ⓑ ⓒ ⓓ   25 ⓐ ⓑ ⓒ ⓓ

Lesson A   *My dad's a salesman.*

Warm-up

 A   Look at the family tree below. Complete the missing labels using the words in the box. Listen and check your answers.

> sister   grandmother   cousin   mother   aunt   grandfather   uncle   father   brother

═══════ married to   ⬭ male   ⬭ female

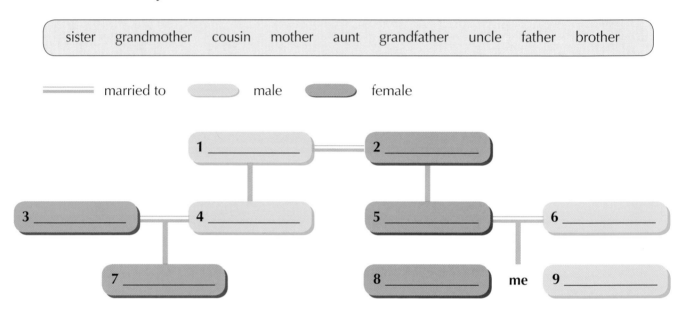

1 _____   2 _____

3 _____   4 _____   5 _____   6 _____

7 _____   8 _____   me   9 _____

B   On a piece of paper, draw a family tree for yourself. Write the names of your family members. Explain your family tree to a partner.

Listening

 A   Hiro is talking about a picture of his family. Number the family members in order (1–5).

B   Circle the extra information he gives about each person.

1 a likes gardening   b not very happy
2 a no job   b salesman
3 a plays catch   b plays in the backyard
4 a high school student   b junior high school student
5 a loves hiking   b loves mountain biking

Further Listening

A Four people are talking about people in their family. Who is each speaker talking about?

1	**a** aunt	**b** mother	**3**	**a** uncle	**b** father
2	**a** brother	**b** cousin	**4**	**a** grandmother	**b** aunt

B Listen again. Circle the picture that best describes the family member.

a   b

a   b

a   b

a   b

Language Focus: *Yes/no questions*

▸ Yes/no questions usually begin with words like: *Will   Can   Does   Do   Is*

    Example: **A:** Does your father have a hobby?
                    B: Yes. He likes playing golf.

C Listen to the conversations again. Which word does each speaker use to begin the yes/no questions?

Question word

1	does	will	can	is	**3**	does	will	can	is
2	does	will	can	is	**4**	does	will	can	is

Talk It Over

Work with a partner.
Ask your partner about his
or her family.

> *Do you have any brothers or sisters?*

> *Yeah, I have a younger brother and an older sister.*

Lesson B — *Wow, you have a lot of CDs!*

Before You Listen

A   Look at this list of places in a house. Check (✔) the ones in your home.

garden	○	living room	○
bedroom	○	kitchen	○
bathroom	○	dining room	○
balcony	○	garage	○
basement	○	attic	○

B   Answer the questions about your home. Compare your answers with a partner's.

1   How many bedrooms are there in your house?
2   Is your bedroom big or small?
3   How many bathrooms are there in your house?
4   Do you have a big living room?

Extended Listening

A   Jimmy is showing his friends around his bedroom. Number the areas of the room they talk about.

B   Listen again. Circle the correct answer.

1   Jimmy uses his computer to . . .   **a** study.   **b** play games.
2   Jimmy uses his telescope . . .   **a** every day.   **b** a few times a week.
3   The fish tank is . . .   **a** easy to take care of.   **b** difficult to take care of.
4   Jimmy spends more time . . .   **a** listening to music.   **b** studying.

Conversation Strategy: *Introducing a question with "So, . . ."*

▸ Speakers sometimes use "So, . . ." to introduce a question, to continue the topic, or to start a new topic.

Example:

A: Do you have your own TV?
B: Yes, I do.
A: So, do you watch TV often?

A: What did you do yesterday?
B: Oh, I went to the mall with Sarah.
A: Yeah? So, did you buy anything?

C Listen to the conversation again. Number these sentences 1–4.

a ___ So, does it help you study?

b ___ So, you listen to a lot of music over here, don't you?

c ___ So, do you use it much?

d ___ So, you don't have to spend a lot of time with it?

Catch It!: Intonation for questions

A This intonation (⌣◢) requires the listener to give a yes or no response.

Do you have a big bedroom? (No, I don't.)

This intonation (⌢◣) requires the listener to make a choice.

Do you have a big bedroom or a small bedroom? (I have a small room.)

B Listen. Decide if you can answer yes or no or if you have to make a choice. Check the boxes.

	1	2	3	4	5	6
Yes or No						
Make a choice						

Try It Out!

Read the questions. Write one more "make a choice" question and one more "yes/no" question of your own. Work with two partners. Ask your partners the questions. Circle their answers.

Question	Partner 1	Partner 2
Does your kitchen have a table?	yes no	yes no
Do you have your own bedroom?	yes no	yes no
_____	yes no	yes no
Do you live in a house or an apartment?	house / apartment	house / apartment
Do you eat in the kitchen or the dining room?	kitchen / dining room	kitchen / dining room
_____	_____ / _____	_____ / _____

Classmates

Lesson A *What's he look like?*

Warm-up

A Look at the four people. How can you describe them? Write 1–4 next to each description below. Each description may fit more than one person. Listen and check your answers.

 ❶

❷

❸

❹

Height:	tall _____ average _____ short _____
Weight:	thin _____ average _____ heavy _____
Hair length:	balding _____ short _____ medium _____ long _____
Hair style:	straight _____ curly _____
Hair color:	blond(e) _____ brown _____ black _____ red _____
Eye color:	blue _____ brown _____ green _____
Skin color:	fair _____ dark _____ tanned _____

B Use the words above to describe yourself. Compare with a partner. Does your partner agree with your description?

> *I'm tall and thin.*

> *I have short, straight, black hair and brown eyes.*

Listening

 A A salesperson is describing the new Nina doll. Listen and number the features the person talks about (1–5).

height ☐   eyes ☐   hair ☐

weight ☐   skin color ☐

a   b   c

B Listen again. Which of the pictures shows Nina?

Further Listening

A Listen to five conversations of people making choices.
Number the pictures in order (1–5).

a ☐ b ☐ c ☐ d ☐ e ☐

B Listen again. Which person is chosen in each conversation?

1	**a** Tyler	**b** Kristy		**4**	**a** Brian	**b** Philip
2	**a** Haruna	**b** Becky		**5**	**a** Alvin	**b** Chika
3	**a** Alex	**b** Seung-Hyun				

Language Focus: *Comparing people*

▶ To compare two people, we can say *X is _____-er than Y* or *X is more _____ than Y.*
heavy → heavier, tall → taller, fashionable → more fashionable

Example: A: Wang Chung is darker than Keiko.
B: Sung-Taek is more handsome than Sean.

C Listen again. Circle the correct option in each sentence.

1 Tyler's hair is longer than / shorter than Kristy's.
2 Haruna's eyes are bigger than / smaller than Becky's.
3 Alex's skin is darker than / lighter than Seung-Hyun's.
4 Brian is thinner than / heavier than Philip.
5 Alex is taller than / shorter than Chika.

Talk It Over

Work with a partner. Choose pairs
of people in your class and make
comparisons. Does your partner agree?

Michelle is more fashionable than Kenji.

No. Kenji is more fashionable.

Before You Listen

A   Match the words in the box to the pictures.

| **a** spots | **b** loose/baggy | **c** tight | **d** plaid | **e** holes | **f** striped | **g** solid |

1 ☐   2 ☐   3 ☐   4 ☐

5 ☐   6 ☐   7 ☐

B   What do you like to wear? Circle the styles you like. Compare your answers with a partner's.

Extended Listening

A   Spike and his friends are watching people at the shopping mall.
Listen and number (1–4) the people he describes.

a ☐   b ☐   c ☐   d ☐

B   Listen again. Who does Spike think is fashionable? Write F (fashionable) or U (unfashionable)
next to each picture.

▸ Listeners sometimes repeat the question to get time to think.

Example:
A: Are those jeans in style?
B: Are they in style? Well, I guess so . . .

C Listen to the conversation again. Which question is repeated?

1 **a** Is that in fashion?   **b** Is that in style?
2 **a** That's no good?   **b** Those are no good?
3 **a** Is that OK?   **b** Are those OK?
4 **a** Are jeans out?   **b** Are jeans in?

Catch It!: Breaking sentences into chunks

A Listen to this sentence from Spike's talk:

She's very fashionable, and she knows it.

Notice how there is a short pause where the comma is in the sentence.

B Mark where commas (,) should appear in these sentences. Listen for pauses and check your answers.

1 Her blouse is white and white goes with anything.
2 This time next year all the girls will copy her style.
3 Tight T-shirts are the newest style not the loose kind.
4 This is a shopping mall not a beach.
5 Would you like the black shirt or the blue one?

Try It Out!

Read the questions below and then write two of your own questions.
Work with a partner. Ask and answer the questions.

Is that a new shirt?
Are those shoes expensive?
Does that <u>shirt</u> match those <u>pants</u>?
Are you interested in fashion?
If you have money, what clothes will you buy?

_____

_____

Is that a new shirt?

New? No, it's old.

Lesson A *Chuck's a really cool guy!*

Warm-up

 A Here are some activities that people do in their free time. Listen. Add four new activities of your own.

reading comics   studying
watching movies   _____
going out to eat   _____
riding a bike   _____
taking photos   _____

 B What do you like doing with your friends? Circle the activities you enjoy from the list above. Tell your partner.

I really like watching movies.

Yeah, me too.

Listening

 A Four people are talking about their best friends. Number the friends in the order they're talked about.

a □   b □   c □   d □

B Listen again. Check (✓) what each speaker says about his or her friends.

1 ___ likes shopping   ___ likes reading
2 ___ lives far from school   ___ lives close to school
3 ___ always neat and clean   ___ likes ice cream
4 ___ from neighborhood   ___ from high school

Further Listening

 A Listen to the conversations. What do the friends enjoy doing together?
Circle the correct picture.

❶

a

b

❸

a

b

❷

a

b

❹

a

b

B Listen again. Circle yes (Y) or no (N).

1 They usually have money.	Y / N	**3** She often uses the camera.	Y / N
2 The movie theater is their favorite place	Y / N	**4** They don't like eating at restaurants.	Y / N

Language Focus: *like/enjoy + verb*

▸ When talking about an activity, speakers often use phrases in the form of *like/enjoy + –ing*
verb.

Example: I **enjoy** sing**ing** karaoke.
I **like** go**ing** shopping.

C Listen again. Which gerund did they use? Circle the word.

Verb	Gerund	Verb	Gerund
1 like	watching / seeing	**3** like	taking / making
2 enjoy	going to / playing	**4** enjoy	eating / cooking

Talk It Over

Work with a partner. Ask what
he or she likes doing.

Do you like singing karaoke?

Yeah, I do.

Before You Listen

 A Complete the sentences below using the words in the box. Listen and check.

> friendly   talkative   funny   shy   serious   kind

1 Keiko's so _____. She almost never talks in groups
   of people. Ian is the opposite. He's really _____.
   He never stops talking!
2 Christine is great at telling jokes. I wish I was
   as _____ as her! I think I'm too _____.
3 My aunt has nine cats. She's so _____ to animals.
4 Jin-Soo is so _____ to everyone.
   He makes friends really easily.

B Put a plus (+) next to two words that describe you. Put a minus (–) next to two words that
don't describe you. Show your words to a partner. Does he or she agree with you?

Extended Listening

 A Keiko is showing her aunt pictures of Keiko's three best friends. Listen to Keiko's
descriptions. Number the friends 1–3.

a ☐

b ☐

c ☐

B   How does Keiko describe each friend? Write T (Tamika), C (Charlotte), or Y (Yoshi) next to each word.

serious ___   smart ___   outgoing ___   talkative ___   shy ___   kind ___

Conversation Strategy: *Getting time to think*

> ▸ Before speakers answer a question, sometimes they need time to think about the answer.
> They often use these phrases before they answer.
>
> *Hmmm . . .*   *Let me think . . .*   *Let me see . . .*   *That's a good question . . .*

C   Listen again. Which phrases does Keiko use in the conversation?
Put them in the order you hear them.

__ Let me see . . .   __ Hmmm . . .   __ Let me think . . .   __ That's a good question . . .

Catch It!: The sound /θ/

A   English learners often have a hard time pronouncing /th/ sounds. Listen to the example.

Example: a thin   **b** sin

B   Listen. Which word do you hear? Circle a or b.

1 a three	**b** tree			**4 a** think	**b** sink		
2 a bath	**b** bus			**5 a** thumb	**b** some		
3 a with	**b** whiz			**6 a** mouth	**b** mouse		

Try It Out!

Add two questions to the chart below. Work with two partners. Ask your partners the questions and write down their answers.

Examples:

A: Who's your best friend?   **A:** What's she like?   **A:** What do you like doing together?
B: My best friend is Mika.   **B:** She's friendly and kind.   **B:** We like listening to music.

Question	Partner 1	Partner 2
Who's your best friend? What's she like? What do you like doing together? _____ _____		

Holidays

10

Lesson A *Let's go!*

Warm-up

 A Here are some activities people do on vacation. Match the pictures with the words in the box. Listen and check.

> **1** cycling   **2** camping   **3** swimming   **4** diving   **5** hiking   **6** snowboarding

a   b   c   d   e   f

B Check the activities you like to do. Compare your answers with a partner's.

Listening

 A Four people are talking about what they like to do in different seasons. Listen and number the seasons in the order you hear them (1–4).

spring ___   summer ___   fall ___   winter ___

B What activity does each person like to do? Circle the correct activity.

1

a   b

3

a   b

2

a   b

4

a   b

Further Listening

A Listen to the short conversations. Circle the activity they are talking about.

1 **a** snowboarding   **b** skateboarding
2 **a** fishing   **b** bowling
3 **a** roller skating   **b** skiing
4 **a** billiards   **b** swimming
5 **a** clothes shopping   **b** eating at a restaurant

B Listen again. When will they do the activity?

1 **a** 10:00 a.m.   **b** 10:00 p.m.
2 **a** tomorrow afternoon   **b** this afternoon
3 **a** Saturday   **b** Sunday
4 **a** tomorrow morning   **b** tonight
5 **a** next week   **b** this weekend

Language Focus: *Inviting*

▸ You can use these phrases to invite someone to do something:

Let's . . .   go skiing.
Do you want to . . .   go swimming tomorrow?
Why don't we . . .   play tennis next week?

C Listen to the conversations again. Which phrases do the speakers use? Check (✔) the boxes.

	1	2	3	4	5
Let's go					
Do you want to go					
Why don't we go					

Talk It Over

Work with a partner. Invite your partner to do an activity with you. Take turns.

Let's go horseback riding!

OK, sounds good!

Before You Listen

 A   Match the picture to the season. Listen and check.

> **1** winter   **2** spring   **3** summer   **4** autumn/fall

c ☐

a ☐

b ☐

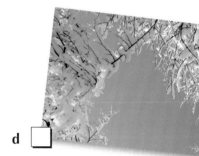

d ☐

B   Answer these questions with a partner.

Which months are winter in North America and Europe?   _____

Which months are autumn in New Zealand and Australia?   _____

1 December January February   **3** June July August

2 March April May   **4** September October November

Extended Listening

 A   Two students are in a photo booth. Number the seasons 1–3 (one season is not used).

   a summer ___   **b** fall ___   **c** winter ___

B   Listen again. Which photograph do they choose for each season? Check (✔) **a** or **b**.

Winter

Summer

a ☐

b ☐

a ☐

b ☐

Fall

a ☐

b ☐

▶ When speakers want to ask their partner the same question their partner just asked, they often use these phrases:

How about you?   *What about you?*

C Listen again. When the speaker says "How about you?" or "What about you?" what does he or she mean? Check the question they are asking.

1 **a** Do you like ice-skating?   **b** Is winter your favorite?
2 **a** Do you like the beach?   **b** Do you like swimming in the ocean?
3 **a** Is spring OK?   **b** Do you like that?

Catch It!: *What/How about you?*

 A Listen to these two sentences with "How about you?" and "What about you?". Each sentence is said twice. In normal conversation, the second way sounds more natural than the first.

I like that one. How about you?   I love summer. What about you?

B Listen and check (✔) the question the speaker asks.

	1	2	3	4	5	6
How about you?						
What about you?						

Try It Out!

Answer the questions. Then ask your partner. Write your partner's answer.

Example:

A: Which month do you want to go skating?
B: I want to go skating in July. How about you?
A: Me too.

A: Which season do you want to go camping?
B: I want to go camping in fall. What about you?
A: I want to go in spring.

Which month do you want to go . . . ?	Me	Partner
skating		
hiking		
biking		
driving		

Which season is best for . . . ?	Me	Partner
watching nature		
swimming		
camping		
snowboarding		

11

Dating

Lesson A *What kind of guy?*

Warm-up

 A Connect each word with its opposite. Listen and check.

funny	lazy
unfriendly	shy/quiet
boring	rude
active	serious
polite	interesting
talkative	friendly

B How about you? Circle six words above that describe you.

Listening

 A Listen to four people describing themselves. Number the speakers in the order you hear them.

a ☐ b ☐ c ☐ d ☐

B What does each person say about his or her personality? Circle **a** or **b**.

1 **a** fun to be with   **b** funny
2 **a** quiet   **b** shy
3 **a** intelligent   **b** serious
4 **a** friendly   **b** crazy

Further Listening

A Four people are talking to the people in the previous activity.
What kind of date do they suggest? Circle **a** or **b**.

1

a   b

3

a   b

2

a   b

4

a   b

B Listen again. Does the person accept or refuse the invitation?

	1	2	3	4
Accept				
Refuse				

Language Focus: *Accepting and refusing invitations*

▸ To accept invitations, use these phrases:
   Sure!   *OK.*   *That sounds good.*
▸ To refuse invitations, people often use phrases that are a little longer:
   Sorry, but I'm busy that day.   *Well, let me think about it.*   *Um, maybe another time.*

C Listen again. Number the phrases in the order you hear them.

   a Uh, well, maybe another time. _____   **c** Well, let me think about it. _____
   b That sounds great. _____   **d** OK. _____

Talk It Over

Work with some partners.
Find out what personality
type your partners like.

What kind of person do you like?

*I like girls who are talkative.
How about you?*

Before You Listen

A Look at the list of things to do on a date. Put them in order from
1 (most interesting) to 9 (most boring).

___ Watch fireworks. ___ Go shopping.
___ Picnic in the park with friends. ___ Go to the movies.
___ Go for a walk. ___ Go to a concert.
___ Have a barbecue party. ___ Study together.
___ Go to dinner.

B Show your list to a partner. Are your lists the same?

Extended Listening

 A Michael is on a TV dating show to choose a date with one of three girls.
Listen and number the girls (1–3).

B Listen again and write T for *True* or F for *False*.

1 Girl #1 wants to go to his favorite restaurant. ____
2 Michael doesn't like watching movies. ____
3 Girl #2 likes sports. ____

4 Michael likes romantic walks ____
5 Girl #3 doesn't have much money. ____

Conversation Strategy: *Making suggestions*

▸ People sometimes use the phrase "How about . . . ?" to make a suggestion.

C Listen again. The phrase "How about . . . ?" is used five times during the game show. Write the missing word in each question.

a How about dinner and a _____?
b How about long, romantic walks in the _____?
c How about _____ pro wrestling?
d How about flying in my private _____?
e How about a _____ on the first date?

Catch It!: *Can vs. can't*

 A *Can* and *can't* aren't usually stressed in conversation, so they're hard to catch. Usually speakers say *can't* with a long vowel sound. Listen to the examples.

I can go to the picnic this weekend.   I can't go skiing tomorrow.

B Listen. Does the speaker say *can* or *can't*. Circle the correct answer.

1	can	can't	**4**	can	can't
2	can	can't	**5**	can	can't
3	can	can't	**6**	can	can't

Try It Out!

Ask someone for a date. Write five activities for "dream dates" in the table below. Then practice with your partner.

Example:

A: Let's go to the beach to watch fireworks next week.
B: Um, I can't go next week. Maybe another time.

A: How about dinner at a restaurant?
B: Sure! That sounds good.

Activity	Partner
	Accept / Refuse
	Accept / Refuse
	Accept / Refuse
	Accept / Refuse
	Accept / Refuse

My Future

12

Lesson A   *I want to be a TV star!*

Warm-up

 A   Match the pictures to the jobs. Listen and check.

| **1** athlete | **2** musician | **3** teacher | **4** radio DJ | **5** company president |

a   b   c   d   e

B   Which of the jobs above would you like to do the most in your future?
What other jobs would you like to do? Tell a partner.

Listening

 A   Listen to the people describing their jobs. Number the pictures in the order you hear them.

a   b   c   d

 B   Listen again. What does each person like about his or her job? Circle **a** or **b**.

1 **a** meet many people   **b** not so busy
2 **a** work inside   **b** work outside
3 **a** enjoy singing   **b** travel to many places
4 **a** help people   **b** enjoy working

Further Listening

A   Listen and match the speakers to their dream jobs.

a owner of small business   **b** designer   **c** reporter   **d** TV star   **e** president of big travel agency

Randy   Jong-Soo   Tamika   Maria   Megumi
1   2   3   4   5

B   Listen again. Why do they want these jobs? Complete the sentences.

1   I can help _____.
2   It would be _____ to be famous.
3   I love _____!

4   To make people's _____ come true.
5   To create a new _____.

Language Focus: *Hope/want + to . . .*

▸ When people talk about their plans for the future, they sometimes use phrases like these:
   I hope to play baseball.   ***I want to*** fly an airplane.

C   Listen to the conversations again. What does each person hope to do? Circle **a** or **b**.

1   **a** write a news story   **b** own a newspaper
2   **a** make a lot of money   **b** make people laugh
3   **a** have a lot of pets   **b** own a small business
4   **a** become rich   **b** travel around the world
5   **a** travel around the world.   **b** change the fashion world

Talk It Over

Work with a partner.
Ask your partner about his
or her hopes for the future.

What do you want to do in the future?

I hope to travel around the world.

Lesson B. *You get three wishes!*

Before You Listen

 A Match the adjectives to the pictures. Listen and check.

| 1 intelligent | 2 rich | 3 talented | 4 happy | 5 popular | 6 beautiful | 7 healthy |

a   b   c   d   e   f   g

B What do you want to be? Circle three from above.

Extended Listening

 A Three girls are on a beach where they find a genie in a bottle. Listen and match each person to her wish.

1	Daphne	to be rich
2	Chloe	to be popular
3	Briana	to be intelligent

B Listen again. What will they do with their wishes? Choose **a** or **b**.

Daphne will:	**a** buy expensive clothes	**b** give money to the poor
Chloe will:	**a** get a new boyfriend	**b** teach everyone about world problems
Briana will:	**a** build a machine	**b** study science and medicine

---

Conversation Strategy: *Showing excitement*

▸ You can use these phrases to show you are excited about something:

Wow! *That's great!* *Unbelievable!* *You're kidding!*

C Listen to the conversations again. Number the expressions 1–5. One is extra.

___ Wow!   ___ That's amazing!   ___ Unbelievable!
___ That's great!   ___ I wish I were you!   ___ You're kidding!

Catch It!: Reduced forms of *want to* and *going to*

A Listen to how "I want to" and "I'm going to" are pronounced in spoken English.

I want to be rich in the future.
I'm going to have my own company one day.

B Listen. Does each speaker say want to or going to? Check (✔) the correct box.

	1	2	3	4	5
want to					
going to					

Try It Out!

The genie has given you three wishes. Write your wishes and the reason why below. Work with a partner. Tell your partner your wishes and ask your partner about his or her wishes.

My wishes:

Wish	Reason
example: To be rich	to fly around the world

My partner's wishes:

Wish	Reason

Practice Test

Part 1

Listen. Choose the best answer.

1 Who are they talking about?

a

c

b

d

2 What does his mother do?

a

c

b

d

3 Which one is her room?

a

b

c

d

4 Which one is his room?

a

b

c

d

5 Which girl do they talk about?

a

b

c

d

6 Which one is in fashion?

a

b

c

d

Listen. Choose the best reply.

7 **a** The one in the black cap.   **c** I like his fashion sense.

   b No, I don't like him.   **d** Next week is better.

8 **a** She should wear heels.   **c** I should be fashionable.

   b She thinks so.   **d** I won't change my fashion.

9 **a** I like her very much.   **c** I copy her fashion.

   b She likes you.   **d** She is very fashionable.

10 **a** We went to the same school.   **c** We like each other.

   b We have the same bags.   **d** We want to know each other.

11 **a** Who is younger?   **c** How does he look?

   b How old is he?   **d** Who do you like?

12 **a** What does she like?   **c** What does he like?

   b What's she like?   **d** What's he like?

13 **a** I usually go to school.   **c** I spend time with my friends.

   b I like my friends.   **d** I should always study.

Part 3

A   Listen. Choose the best answer.

14   Where are they going?

    a the sea   **b** the mountains   **c** a concert   **d** school

15   What are they going to do?

    a They are going swimming.   **c** They are going to his mother's place.

    b They are going home.   **d** They are going shopping.

16   When does the boy like to visit the zoo?

    a in spring   **b** in summer   **c** in fall   **d** in winter

B   Listen. Choose the best answer (a–f) for questions 17–19.

Schedule

Wednesday	Thursday	Friday	Saturday	Sunday	Monday	Tuesday
		17	18	19		

    a Swimming   **d** Cycling

    b Skating   **e** Having a romantic date

    c Camping   **f** Having a party

Part 4

A   Listen. Choose the best answer.

20 What does he look like?

    a He is tall and handsome with long brown hair and blue eyes.

    b He is tall and handsome with short blond hair and blue eyes.

    c He is tall and handsome with long blond hair and brown eyes.

    d He is tall and handsome with long brown hair and brown eyes.

21 What can he do well?

    a ski   **b** snowboard   **c** skate and ski   **d** ski and snowboard

22 What did the girl do on her summer vacation?

    a went to Disneyland and Universal Studios

    b went to Disneyland and played tennis

    c went to Universal Studios

    d played tennis

B   Listen. Choose the best answer.

23 What did many famous people have when they were young?

    a money   **b** dreams   **c** sports   **d** music

24 Why did the boy give up his first dream?

    a He couldn't play the guitar well.

    b He was too short.

    c He liked music better than sports.

    d He wanted to be famous.

25 What did the boy learn?

    a Don't work hard.   **b** Don't give up.   **c** To dream hard.   **d** To study lessons.

Practice Test 2 Answer Sheet

Part 1

1 (a) (b) (c) (d)   4 (a) (b) (c) (d)
2 (a) (b) (c) (d)   5 (a) (b) (c) (d)
3 (a) (b) (c) (d)   6 (a) (b) (c) (d)

Part 2

7 (a) (b) (c) (d)   11 (a) (b) (c) (d)
8 (a) (b) (c) (d)   12 (a) (b) (c) (d)
9 (a) (b) (c) (d)   13 (a) (b) (c) (d)
10 (a) (b) (c) (d)

Part 3

14 (a) (b) (c) (d)   17 (a) (b) (c) (d) (e) (f)
15 (a) (b) (c) (d)   18 (a) (b) (c) (d) (e) (f)
16 (a) (b) (c) (d)   19 (a) (b) (c) (d) (e) (f)

Part 4

A   **B**
20 (a) (b) (c) (d)   23 (a) (b) (c) (d)
21 (a) (b) (c) (d)   24 (a) (b) (c) (d)
22 (a) (b) (c) (d)   25 (a) (b) (c) (d)

Introduction to the Self-Study Units

Everyone needs more listening practice. So, after you finish each unit, go to the self-study section. Listen to the CD in the back of the book and take the 10-point quiz.

Sometimes you'll fill in the missing words. Sometimes you'll answer questions. Write your answers on the side of the page.

The CD is yours, so listen as many times as you want!

Good luck!!

Self-Study

A Listen. Choose the correct answer.

TRACK 1

Total ____

Clerk:	Hi, what's your name?	
Customer:	My name is **a** Kathy ₁ **b** Cassie.	**1** ___
Clerk:	Where do you live?	
Customer:	I live in **a** Tuwell ₂ **b** Sewell City.	**2** ___
Clerk:	I see. What is your address?	
Customer:	My address is 1526 **a** Morse ₃ **b** Moore Street.	**3** ___
Clerk:	OK, thanks. Do you have an e-mail address?	
Customer:	Yes, it's **a** kllrpr@thommail.com ₄ **b** krklpr@thommail.com.	**4** ___
Clerk:	I need your last name, too.	
Customer:	Sure, It's **a** L-I-M ₅ **b** R-I-M.	**5** ___
Clerk:	And your phone number, please.	
Customer:	**a** 363-6023 ₆ **b** 336-6023.	**6** ___
Clerk:	OK. Thank you.	

B Listen. Choose the correct answer.

TRACK 2

7 What's her friend's name?

   a Mickey   **c** Nathan

   b Nancy   **d** Nicky

7 ___

8 What is her e-mail address?

   a matoya@kert.com   **c** matoya@kelt.com

   b natoya@kart.com   **d** magoya@kalt.com

8 ___

9 Where does he live now?

   a 226 Ork Street   **c** 260 Lark Street

   b 266 Ork Street   **d** 264 Lark Street

9 ___

10 What's the man's phone number?

   a 482-8673   **c** 428-8673

   b 428-8763   **d** 482-8763

10 ___

Self-Study

Total ____

1 ___

2 ___

3 ___

4 ___

5 ___

A Listen. Choose the correct answer.

TRACK 3

Ken: Hi, what's up?

Jenny: I woke up really late this morning.

Ken: Yeah? What time did you get up?

Jenny: I woke up at **a** 6:15 ₁ **b** 6:50.

Ken: Oh, that's not so late.

Jenny: Yeah, but I usually wake up at **a** 6:15 ₂ **b** 6:50.

Ken: Really?

Jenny: How about you? What time do you usually wake up?

Ken: I get up at **a** 7:30 ₃ **b** 7:13.

Jenny: Really? Why is that?

Ken: Because that's exactly when my favorite TV program starts.

Jenny: Ah hah. Which channel?

Ken: It's channel **a** 12 ₄ **b** 20.

Jenny: OK, I'll try to watch it tomorrow.

Ken: You can't! Remember, you have to leave your house at **a** 7:15 ₅ **b** 7:00.

6 ___

7 ___

8 ___

9 ___

10 ___

B Listen. Choose the best response.

TRACK 4

6 a Can I call your number?　　　　**c** Can I call your mother?

b Can I have your phone number?　　**d** Say your mother's number.

7 a OK, Monday the 27th.　　　　　**c** OK, Monday the 22nd.

b OK, Monday the 12th.　　　　　**d** OK, Monday the 21st.

8 a Give me your name.　　　　　　**c** Can I have your present?

b Give me your number.　　　　　　**d** What's your name?

9 a Sure, Tuesday the 12th.　　　　　**c** Sure, Thursday the 20th.

b Sure, Tuesday the 12th.　　　　　**d** Sure, Thursday the 12th.

10 a What's the address?　　　　　　**c** What's your name?

b What's your telephone number?　　**d** When is it?

A   Listen. Write the missing words.

Total ____

> **a** sometimes   **b** walk   **c** always   **d** drive   **e** usually   **f** never

A: Hi, I didn't know you take this bus.

B: Yeah, I **1** _____ take this bus. Do you take this bus every day, too?

A: Yeah, but I **2** _____ walk two bus stops, then catch this bus.

B: Oh, I see.

A: How about Saturdays when you play soccer?

B: I usually **3** _____ to school.

A: Really?

B: Because we don't have many buses on weekends and it's good exercise.

A: Yeah? I **4** _____ do that.

B: Do you do any sport?

A: I **5** _____ play tennis with my friends at the park.

1 ___
2 ___

3 ___

4 ___

5 ___

 B   Listen. Choose the correct answer.

6 How does the girl go to school?
  a on foot   **c** on foot and by bus
  b by bus   **d** by train

7 How long does it take him to clean his room?
  a thirty minutes   **c** ninety minutes
  b one hour   **d** three hours

8 When does she usually do her homework?
  a in the morning   **c** in the afternoon
  b at lunch   **d** at night

9 What does he borrow from the library?
  a books only   **c** always books and DVDs
  b DVDs only   **d** always DVDs and sometimes books

10 How does the girl usually go to school when it rains?
  a by bike   **c** by car
  b by train   **d** on foot

6 ___

7 ___

8 ___

9 ___

10 ___

Self-Study

Total ____

A Listen. Complete the sentences using the words in the box. Two words are extra.

TRACK 7

> **a** right **b** at **c** on
> **d** across from **e** left **f** next to

1 ___

A: Excuse me, do you know where City Hall is?

B: I'm sorry, I don't know. Why don't you ask the police officer **1** _____ the corner?

A: Yeah thanks . . . Excuse me, can you tell me where City Hall is?

2 ___

C: Sure, go down this street, turn **2** _____,

3 ___

and it's on the **3** _____.

4 ___

A: 4 _____ the library?

B: That's right.

A: Thank you.

B Listen. Where is each item? Match the items and the places.

TRACK 8

5 ___   **5** cell phone   **a** in the dictionary

6 ___   **6** blue bag   **b** behind the bed

7 ___   **7** watch   **c** behind the TV

8 ___   **8** wallet   **d** under the bed

9 ___   **9** dictionary   **e** on the TV

10 ___   **10** money   **f** in the bag

A   Listen. Choose the best answer.

Total ____

TRACK
9

A: Let's go to see that new movie.

B: I just saw it yesterday.

A: Well, how about going **a** shopping ₁ **b** skating?

1 ___

B: I don't have much money.

A: Yeah, me neither. Would you like to **a** go swimming ₂ **b** go walking?

2 ___

B: Oh, I **a** really don't like ₃ **b** don't like that. Maybe we could read comics at
your place.

3 ___

A: a Good idea. ₄ **b** That's great.

4 ___

 B   Listen. Answer the questions. (Each question is two points.)

TRACK
10

5 What does the speaker like to do?

5 ___

    a nothing   **c** jog

    b walk   **d** buy shoes

6 What season does the speaker like the most?

6 ___

    a spring   **c** fall

    b summer   **d** winter

7 What does the speaker do on Sundays?

7 ___

    a sing karaoke   **c** sleep

    b spend time with her classmates   **d** dance

Self-Study

Total ____

 A

TRACK 11

Listen. Complete the sentences using the words in the box. Four words are extra.

> **a** present   **b** shoes   **c** cheap   **d** always
>
> **e** often   **f** price   **g** comfortable   **h** shirt

1 ___

2 ___

3 ___

4 ___

A: Ooh, that's nice. I like your **1** _____.

B: Oh this thing? Thanks. I **2** _____ wear it.

A: It's really cute.

B: You think so? I'll tell you, it's so **3** _____.

A: Oh, really? It looks a little expensive.

B: You're kidding. To tell the truth, it was **4** _____.

B

TRACK 12

Listen. Answer the three questions about the talk. (Each question is two points.)

5 ___

5 What is easy to wear?

   a sneakers   **c** bracelets

   b jeans   **d** rings

6 ___

6 What do teenagers <u>often</u> wear?

   a rings   **c** earrings

   b sneakers   **d** bracelets

7 ___

7 What teenagers <u>always</u> do?

   a wear jeans   **c** read fashion magazines

   b wear rings and bracelets   **d** talk about fashion

 A   Listen. Choose the best answer.

TRACK
13

Total ___

A: Let me see your pictures. Who's this?

B: This is my father. He's a **a** doctor ₁ **b** salesperson.

A: Oh. Does he play any sports?

B: No, but he likes watching **a** baseball ₂ **b** soccer.

A: And is this your grandmother? She looks very **a** healthy ₃ **b** pretty.

B: Yeah, she swims three times a week.

A: Is that her hobby?

B: No, she likes to play **a** games ₄ **b** tennis.

A: I see. And this?

B: Oh, that's my big brother. He's a **a** painter ₅ **b** carpenter.

A: But I saw him at school the other day.

B: Yeah, he goes to school to coach **a** swimming ₆ **b** basketball.

A: That's nice.

1 ___

2 ___

3 ___

4 ___

5 ___

6 ___

 B   Listen. Choose the correct picture. (Each question is two points.)

TRACK
14

7   Which photograph are they talking about?

7 ___

a   b   c   d

8   Which is the woman's room?

8 ___

a   b   c   d

Self-Study

Total ____

1 ____

2 ____

3 ____

4 ____

5 ____

6 ____

 A Listen. Choose the correct answer.

TRACK
15

A: Hey, look at the pictures in this magazine. Which model do you like best?

B: Let me see . . . I like the girl with the **a** shorter $_1$ **b** longer hair.

A: Me, too, but I like **a** black $_2$ **b** brown hair better.

B: Then how about this girl?

A: She's OK, but I like **a** smaller $_3$ **b** bigger eyes.

B: Really? I don't.

A: Which girl do you like best, then?

B: I like her. Because she's so thin.

A: Yeah, she's nice. She has **a** light $_4$ **b** dark hair.

B: So, how are you going to do your hair?

A: Well, I like her, and her, and her, I can't decide. I just want to change my hair
  a color $_5$ **b** style. What about you?

B: Me? But I like my **a** natural $_6$ **b** long hair.

B: Oh, come on!

B Listen. Choose the best response.

TRACK
16

7 ____

8 ____

9 ____

10 ____

7 **a** He's so tall.   **c** Is his hair long?
   b Does he have jeans?   **d** He likes school.

8 **a** Do you know her?   **c** Can I call her?
   b Do you like it?   **d** Can you eat it?

9 **a** Can I wear your jeans?   **c** Not at all.
   b I don't like the dress.   **d** That's a good idea.

10 **a** It looks bad.   **c** Brown is my favorite.
   b It looks great short.   **d** I like it long too.

Self-Study

A Listen. Complete the conversation using the words in the box.

Total ____

TRACK
17

> **a** neighborhood   **b** baseball   **c** games   **d** usually   **e** have fun   **f** study

Grandpa: So, how is your school?
Grandson: It's OK.
Grandpa: Do you have many friends?
Grandson: I have some friends and one really good friend. He and I like to play
       1 _____ together.   **1** ___
Grandpa: How about that? Did you go to the same elementary school?
Grandson: No, but we were in the same **2** _____. He went to a private school.   **2** ___
Grandpa: So, do you spend a lot of time together?
Grandson: Yeah, we play **3** _____ together every day.   **3** ___
       And we **4** _____ spend weekends together, too.   **4** ___
Grandpa: What do you do then?
Grandson: We do lots of things. We just like to **5** _____.   **5** ___
       Do you have good friends?
Grandpa: Of course I do! Friends are very important.

B Listen. Choose the correct answer.

TRACK
18

6 Who is in the picture?   **6** ___
   a sisters   **c** his best friend
   b brother and sister   **d** sister and her best friend

7 What does the new student look like?   **7** ___
   a very friendly   **c** not very serious
   b not very friendly   **d** very talkative

8 Who is coming tomorrow night?   **8** ___
   a the baseball team   **c** his mother's friend
   b the boy's friend   **d** a shy little girl

9 What kind of girl does the boy like?   **9** ___
   a very talkative   **c** funny and outgoing
   b funny and talkative   **d** funny, outgoing, and talkative

10 Why are they going to call Mike?   **10** ___
   a to tell him where to eat   **c** to go to junior high school
   b to invite him   **d** to visit Mike's restaurant

Total ____

 A   Listen. Choose the correct answer.

TRACK
19

1 ___

2 ___

A: What are you doing this summer vacation?

B: I haven't decided yet.

A: Let's go **a** swimming ₁ **b** fishing.

B: That's a **a** good ₂ **b** great idea.

A: Do you know any good places to go?

B: Well, how about Lake Tahoe?

A: That's a good idea.

3 ___

4 ___

5 ___

B: In **a** July ₃ **b** August there's a festival, too.

A: That sounds **a** fun ₄ **b** interesting.

B: Why don't we go to the **a** bookstore ₅ **b** mall to get some information?

A: Yeah, let's go now.

 B   Listen. Complete the schedule using the words in the box.

TRACK
20

a go hiking	**b** go to concerts	**c** have test
d go to Okinawa	**e** go skiing	**f** go to Tokyo

CALENDAR

6 ___

7 ___

8 ___

9 ___

10 ___

JANUARY	FEBRUARY	MARCH	APRIL	MAY	JUNE	JULY	AUGUST
	6	7		8	9		10

Self-Study

A Listen. Choose the correct answer.

TRACK
21

A: Are you free this **a** Sunday ₁ **b** Saturday?

B: Yeah. Why?

A: Can you meet me for **a** dinner ₂ **b** coffee?

B: Yeah, sure.

A: Where shall we meet?

B: **a** In front of ₃ **b** Behind the school?

A: That sounds fine.

B: What time?

A: How about 9:30?

B: Oh, I can't meet that early. How about **a** 12:30 ₄ **b** 11:30?

A: OK, see you then.

B Listen. Answer the questions. (Each question is two points.)

TRACK
22

5 What does her boyfriend do?

　　a play sports　　　　　　**c** write songs

　　b play the piano　　　　　**d** play the piano and write songs

6 Which is NOT her ideal date?

　　a a barbecue　　　　　　**c** talking

　　b staying indoors　　　　 **d** swimming

7 Where can he take her?

　　a to visit his family　　　　**c** a nice restaurant

　　b a fast food place　　　　**d** shopping

Total ____

1 ___

2 ___

3 ___

4 ___

5 ___

6 ___

7 ___

Self-Study

Total ____

1 ___

2 ___

3 ___

4 ___

 A Listen. Choose the correct answer.

TRACK 23

A: What's your dream for the future?

B: Let me see. I want to do something special. I want to be a **a** doctor ₁ **b** reporter.

A: That's great. Why do you want to do that?

B: Well, I want to **a** be famous ₂ **b** help people. That's been my dream for a long time. How about you?

A: Your plan sounds good, but I hope to **a** start a company ₃ **b** see the world.

B: You're kidding! I never knew that. Why?

A: Then I can **a** meet people ₄ **b** see places all over the world.

B: That's a good plan, too. Good luck!

5 ___

6 ___

7 ___

B Listen. Answer the questions about the talk. (Each question is two points.)

TRACK 24

5 What is the speaker talking about?

    a your life   **c** the future

    b dreams   **d** your mind

6 How many dreams should people have?

    a one   **c** three

    b two   **d** many

7 What should you always keep in your mind?

    a something important   **c** your dreams

    b something interesting   **d** small things